Avoiding the 10 Common

CHURCH CRISES

KIRBY CLEMENTS SR.

CLEMENTS FAMILY
MINISTRIES

AVOIDING THE TEN COMMON CHURCH CRISES
Copyright © 2012 by Kirby Clements Sr.

Address inquiries to the publisher:

Clements Family Ministry
2000 Cathedral Place
Decatur, Georgia 30034 USA

Learn more about the author and his ministry at
www.clementsfamilyministry.com

ISBN: 978-0-9794181-8-1

LCCN: 2012950471

First Printing: October 2012

Printed in the United States of America

Edited and composed by Annette R. Johnson,
Allwrite Publishing

TABLE OF CONTENTS

Introduction

The prophet Habakkuk declared that the knowledge of the glory of the Lord will fill the earth. In essence, there shall be a conscious awareness and integration of the invisible attributes of God. Divine power, purpose, priorities, and perspectives shall be seen and expressed. The Church, through its delegated authority and assigned responsibility, is pivotal in the fulfillment of this great commission. However, there have been challenges in the discharge of this function and the battleground has always been conceptual, involving the interpretation and integration of historic truths and events. From apostolic days until this present moment, these challenges to correctly interpreting and implementing historic truth have emerged in areas of government, worship, commission, theology, and sociology of the Church. That is, conflicts over Divine purposes, priorities, and perspectives have often been expressed in these areas of Church activities.

Reformation has been the heavenly response to such times of confusion and disorientation. Reformers have appeared on the scene with ideas, thoughts, and wisdom necessary to readjust the Church. The areas of focus have been theology, worship, governance, and commission. That is, the common challenges have emerged in these ministry functions.

In this work, we shall examine the ten common church crises. They represent the preaching and teaching agenda; building expansion; restoration of the fallen; raising money; ministry philosophy; and others. Ministry has occupational blessings and hazards. The hope is that we can reap the former and avoid the latter.

CRISIS 1

The Subjection of the Holy Spirit

This past century is marked with tremendous revival emphases. Beginning with the Pentecostal Movement of the second half of the 19th century, there followed a series of other movements that has restored principles and practices previously neglected or abandoned by the Church and that reflect the finished work of Christ. The Holy Spirit has reformed our thinking on such issues as the Kingdom of God, spiritual authority, prophecy, evangelism, prayer, healing, deliverance, faith, miracles, covenant, worship, five-fold ministry, body ministry, reconciliation of race and gender, and many others. Over the course of time, there has similarly been an increased awareness of the unity of the Body of Christ, giving rise in some cases to the proliferation of non-denominational churches. Of particular interest, however, is the fact that the Pentecostal/Charismatic dimension of the Church has received greater visibility and credibility. Conferences, television, radio, and other media exposure has brought the person and ministry of the Holy Spirit into the homes, marketplaces, and even the political world where laws and legislation are formed. As the "Spirit-filled" ministries and churches become popular, multitudes join their ranks along with a host of celebrities, entertainers, politicians, professionals, and wealthy entrepreneurs. In order to manage this explosion of growth, there has been the development of ministry programs, organizational structures, and beautiful buildings. Rising cost factors demand that pastors and leaders preach more "vision-driven messages" to enlist the commitment and financial participation of their partners and members.

With such an emphasis on productivity, growth, and efficiency, a subtle anti-Pentecostal/Charismatic sentiment is becoming more noticeable in the churches. Once there was corporate singing of psalms, hymns, spiritual songs, and making of melodies in the hearts of believers; once there was prophetic preaching sprinkled with words of knowledge and wisdom; once there was the manifestation of faith,

miracles, signs, and wonders; and once there was corporate obedience to spiritual directives regarding evangelism and witnessing to the world. Gradually, such spiritual activities have declined as the demand for more acceptability, sophistication, and professionalism becomes greater. Indeed, there is still preaching, teaching, singing, and dancing for two or three hours on a Sunday; and there are still those scheduled "special meetings" for healing, miracles, and celebration. However, congregations and leaders who were once eager participants with the Holy Spirit are degenerating into bands of spectators watching a religious drama or show. The institutionalization of the church with its mounting emphasis on structure, programs, organization, and need for more social acceptability reduces the Holy Spirit to a doctrine, a song, a dance, or even to a "special meeting."

This analogy seems strange, at first, when you consider that a casual glimpse back over the past century reveals such an increase in new ministries, churches, and outreach programs. After all, whenever Christianity becomes a living force, the doctrine of the Holy Spirit receives some primary attention. Yet, how can there be an increase in ministry activities and a decrease in Holy Spirit dynamics? It is because during a century of restoration and the increased popularity of charismatic activities, the Holy Spirit is becoming synonymous with the religious activities and programs.

It is possible that the multitudes have been attracted to "the loaves and fishes" and have missed the personal experience with the One who makes it all possible? In fact, the term "Spirit-filled," which once was used to certify the presence of the Baptism in the Holy Spirit, has since been cast aside in favor of other trendy expressions, such as being "spiritual." To be more specific, when was the last time a message was preached on the person and ministry of the Holy Spirit? Because most church growth has been accomplished, to some degree, through the transfer of memberships from one ministry to another, no one proactively seeks to know from the new members "if God gave them the same gift as He gave us when we believed on the Lord Jesus Christ" (Acts 11:17).

Whenever there is a decline in personal involvement with the person and character of the Holy Spirit, an increase in human activities serves as a camouflage. The words of the prophet may seem to be coarse, but nonetheless true, when he declares, "Forasmuch as this people draw near me with their mouth, and with their lips do honor me, but have removed their heart far from me, and their fear toward me is taught by the precept of men" (Isaiah 29:13). Whenever there is a rise in strife, contention, division, and internal moral and ethical disintegration of ministries, there is a decline in the emphasis on the person and character of the Holy Spirit. Pentecost is the manifestation of power and character.

Ministries are measured by their attendance, programs, publications, musicians, outreach activities, political and social influence, and a host of other factors. And these are wonderful demonstrations of the power of the Christian influence. However, the rising decline in the ethics and the morality of ministries and individual believers raises suspicion concerning the Baptism in the Holy Spirit. Indeed, the Baptism in the Holy Spirit is no substitute for sound doctrine and theological concepts; however, you cannot be intimately involved with Him without experiencing both His fruit and power.

The last century began with the explosion of the Pentecostal Movement and an emphasis upon the baptism and ministration of the Holy Spirit. We witnessed that whenever Christ has become an active power within us, the anointing of Holy Spirit has been highly regarded. It may do us well to refocus upon His person, character, and mission once again.

Historical Perspective

The prophet Joel foretold of the outpouring of the Spirit upon all flesh in latter times (Joel 2:28-29). Luke recorded how an angel revealed to Zacharias that his barren wife, Elizabeth, would bear a son filled with the Holy Spirit, even from his mother's womb (Luke 1:15). Some

months later, when Mary visited her kinswoman Elizabeth, Luke recorded that "when Elizabeth heard the salutation of Mary, the babe leaped in her womb; and Elizabeth was filled with the Holy Spirit" (Luke 1:15). At the birth of John, Zacharias himself "was filled with the Holy Spirit and prophesied" (Luke 1:67). The Holy Spirit, scripture asserts, enabled Zacharias, Elizabeth, John, Mary, and even Simeon and Anna to fulfill their prophetic roles.

Thirty years later, the fulfillment of Joel's prophesy seemed to be at hand. John the Baptist announced that One is coming who "will baptize you in the Holy Spirit and fire" (Luke 3:16). Interestingly, Luke never recorded that John made any reference to the birth, life, ministry, death, or resurrection of the Lord Jesus. Indeed, John announced that Jesus is the "Lamb of God that takes away the sins of the world," but John was clear that when the earthly ministry of Jesus was complete, Joel's prophecy would be fulfilled.

During His ministry, the Lord Jesus revealed to the disciples that another Comforter is coming (John 14:16-18), who will guide them into all truth and bring to their remembrance all things (John 16:13-15). He will convict the world of sin, and of righteousness, and of judgment (John 16:8-11). He will refute all contrary arguments, logic, and wisdom. Currently, the world is surrendered to a foreign power and acts in a manner contrary to its original destiny. The Comforter meanwhile, though, will correct and instruct believers through the ministry of the united redeemed community, or the Church. He will testify through the ministry of the Word and supernatural manifestation that there is only one living and true God and that Jesus Christ is Lord and King.

Luke recorded that the promised event foretold by Joel and the Lord Jesus would take place in Jerusalem. The disciples were to be

empowered with the Spirit in order that they may be "witnesses in Jerusalem, and in all Judea, and Samaria, and to the end of the earth" (Acts 1:8). Jesus commissioned the disciples to be witnesses of Him, the fulfillment of the Scripture in him, his suffering and death, his resurrection, and the proclamation of repentance and faith in his name to all nations (Green, 1970).

The book of Acts records the beginning of this charismatic community. The outpouring of the Holy Spirit upon a small band of believers sparks a revival that gradually turned the world upside down. These early Christians were radically committed to Christ, and they proclaimed the Good News of His life, death, and resurrection with great zeal. There were acts of raw courage and exciting evangelism. These believers were also preoccupied with the presence of the Holy Spirit who revealed Himself in dramatic ways. Miracles, signs, and wonders were magnificent demonstrations of the credibility of the Gospel and the validation of those who preach it. Believers spoke in tongues and prophesied as they were filled with the Spirit (Acts 2:4; 21:9). Judgment was pronounced upon opponents of the Gospel through the Spirit (Acts 13:10-11). The Holy Spirit flowed among and filled the believers, helping them, leading them to maturity, and showing Himself in powerful action (Acts 2:42, 46; 5:42; 1 Cor. 11:20; 14). The Spirit guides (John 16:13; Jam. 1:5), teaches (John 14:26; 1 Cor. 2:7-13), heals (1 Cor. 12:9), delivers (2 Cor. 4:8-18), restores (2 Cor. 12:7-9), and intercedes for believers (John 14:16-17; Rom. 8:26-27). He is seen to be involved in discipleship (John 14:25-26; 15:26-27; 16:12-15); in commission (John 20:19-23); in the diaconate (Acts 6:3-5); in evangelism (Acts 8:15-17; 8:29-39; 9:17; 10:19, 44-47); in the exposure of prejudice (Acts 10:1-48; 11:12-17); in prophetic warnings (Acts 11:28; 20:22-24); in dealing with opposition (Acts 13:9); in validation of ministry (Acts 4:333; 15:7-9; 2 Cor. 12:12); in ministerial directions (Acts 16:6-7); and in the validation of callings (Acts 20:28; 2 Cor. 13:3).

Indeed, world evangelism is a significant purpose of Pentecost. Acts 1-7 records the initial Jerusalem, or Judean, phase. This is followed in chapters 8 and 9 by the record of the Samarian mission. Finally, chapters 10-28 record the details of the apostolic witness to the Gentile world. In time, Christianity in every major New Testament center knew something of the moving of the Spirit. This included Jerusalem, Caesarea, Samaria, Antioch, Ephesus, Colosse, Thessalonica, Corinth, Rome, and the communities to which the book of Hebrews is written. Worship was alive in the Spirit in these places (1 Cor. 14:26-33; Col. 3:16).

Admittedly, there were dangers and extremes from the beginning that triggered a need for moderation and structure in order to unify the diverse elements of the Spirit, such as speaking in tongues and prophecy, on the one hand, and the fixed acts and forms of liturgy on the other (Rom. 12:3-13; 1 Cor. 12). However, Paul was able to unite the breaking of bread, reading, proclamation, confession, prayer, doxology, blessing, hymns, spiritual songs, prophecies, and speaking in tongues with interpretation, so that the freedom of the Spirit and the restraints of liturgy work together for the building of the Church (1 Cor. 14).

While the early church was fairly unified in practice and doctrine, the death of the founding Apostles and disciples, the onslaught of heresies, the infiltration of false teachers, and the inclusions of different cultures threatened this unity. Consequently, efforts were made to consolidate the faith through confessions, creedal statements, catechisms, traditions, and by the elevation of the episcopacy to a place of unquestioned preeminence. Even the idea of apostolic succession emerged as a concept to validate the accuracy and continuity of doctrine and practice. The canons of the first seven Ecumenical Councils from the First Council of Nicaea (325

A.D.) to the Second Council of Nicaea (787 A.D.) represent efforts to reach a consensus in Christian policy and liturgical expressions. However, with this institutionalization of the Church, arose an anti-charismatic sentiment. Augustine further promoted the idea that the supernatural stopped with the apostolic fathers. In the midst of all of this, the gifts of the Spirit seemingly vanished. In fact, by A.D. 260, the charismatic dimension was no longer comfortable in the highly organized, well-educated, wealthy, and socially-powerful Christian communities (Kydd, 1984).

Down through the years, the Holy Spirit has not always received the respect and priority He deserves. During the late 2nd and 3rd century, the church was institutionalized with an emphasis on rules, rights, orders, and dogmas. With such an emphasis, there was a decline in the acknowledgement of gifts of the Holy Spirit. This is most interesting considering the fact that the Church is a worldwide fellowship of the Holy Spirit taking form in various fellowships and congregations of the one Body of Jesus Christ (1 Cor. 12:12-28; Eph. 2:1-22; Col. 1:13-18). Yet with time, the Holy Spirit has been neglected and almost supplanted because of the institutionalization of the Church and other substitutes.

The early creeds, out of necessity to correct heresy, focused upon the person and nature of Christ and gave very little attention to the Holy Spirit. For example, the Apostolic Creed gives very little reference to Him with only the words, *"I believe in the Holy Spirit."* The Nicene Creed only declares, *"We believe in the Holy Spirit, the Lord, the giver of life, who proceeds from the Father and the Son. With the Father and the Son, he is worshiped and glorified. He has spoken through the prophets."* There is no Chalcedon statement, one of the first seven Ecumenical Councils adopted at the Council of Chalcedon in 451 A.D., about the identity of the Spirit. Nevertheless, throughout the Scriptures, the Holy Spirit is symbolically and abundantly represented as the Dove (Matt. 3:16;

10:16), the Oil (Exodus 30:25-38; Lev. 21:10; Luke 4:18; Acts 10:38), the Fire (Exodus 3:2; Mal. 3:2; Matt. 3:11; Acts 2:3), the Rain (Deut. 32:2; Psalm 72:6; Jer. 5:24; Zech. 10:1), the Wind (Isaiah 11:7; Ezek. 37:9; John 3:8; Acts 2:2), the Rivers (Psalm 1:3; 46:4; John 7:38), the Dew (Gen. 27:28; Psalm 133:3; Isaiah 18:4; Hosea 14:5), the Water (Psalm 65:9; Isaiah 44:3; John 3:5; 7:37,38), and even the Clothing (Judges 6:34; Luke 24:49).

Many times afterward, perhaps in response to periods of moral and spiritual decline, there surfaced a revival of charismatic activity, but it was deficient in theological and doctrinal content. Charles W. Conn, in his history of the Church of God, described one of the early revivals:

> *Enthusiasm remained high. The services were generally of an emotional nature, yet the stabilizing influence of teaching, while far from adequate, was not altogether absent. The emotion that made the worshippers weep, laugh, and shout was not some indefinable psychological delirium; it stemmed from the exaltation they received from the sense of the presence of God (Conn, 1977).*

The Presbyterians come under the influence of the Second Great Awakening, which began in the Cane Ridge, Kentucky, area in 1801. William Sweet, in his history of "Revivalism in America," recorded that at the Cane Ridge camp meeting, thousands of people would fall in the state of a trance, and hundreds were given to such demonstrations as "jerking, rolling, dancing, and barking" (Sweet, 1967). A casual visitor to the Azusa Street revival in Los Angeles in the early 20th century would be awestruck by the frenzy of religious zeal, as men and women would shout, dance, speak in tongues, fall into trances, and give interpretation to tongues in English.

Indeed, the outpouring of the Holy Spirit and the enthusiastic

emotional response of people to the presence of God often stimulates more sensationalism than sound theology. However, with the passing of time, an interesting phenomenon has occurred. Efforts have been made to develop sound theology and strategies to accompany the spiritual experiences. As such, the emergence of healing evangelists and mass evangelism has taken the Gospel and the power of the Holy Spirit to the nations (Harrell, 1975). Pentecostals are even building colleges and universities that introduce scholarship to the dynamics of the Holy Spirit (Burgess and McGee, 1987). Eventually, comes a convergence of classic Pentecostal thought and reformed theology, or as we like to say, the "historic Church" and the "present truth Church" finally meet. When the power dynamic of the Holy Spirit is properly mixed with sound theological and doctrinal concepts, there emerges ministries that proclaim and demonstrate the reality of the Kingdom of God as a past, present, and future truth (Paulk and Rhodes, 2000). These churches have congregations who dance and sing in the Spirit, speak in tongues, interpret tongues, prophesy, cast out demons, heal the sick, raise the dead, work miracles, and influence the communities, nations, and even the world.

Once a congregation achieves this proper unity of the Word and the Spirit, something very interesting begins to happen again. The excitement and power of Pentecost begins to wane as the church seeks credibility and popularity through advertising, public relations, television, radio, and the media, which bring tremendous exposure and acceptability. As politicians, entertainers, doctors, lawyers, educators, scientists, athletes, and wealthy entrepreneurs began to join the church, the demand for acceptability and sophistication becomes even greater. At first, the slight decline in spiritual activities is unnoticeable. Indeed, there is preaching or teaching for an hour; musical and dramatic presentations are prevalent; emotionalism runs high, and there is still a consciousness of the Holy Spirit. However, a subtle decline in the Spirit dynamics emerges among the people

beyond the emotional responses to His presence. Where once there was corporate singing of psalms, hymns, spiritual songs, and making melodies in the heart; prophetic preaching sprinkled with words of knowledge and words of wisdom; the manifestation of faith, miracles, and healings; and corporate obedience to spiritual directives regarding giving and receiving, there gradually grows the need for more government, ministry programs, vision-driven messages, and buildings that will attract and manage the masses. These modernizations put a squeeze on the "spiritual" activities. Again, the congregations who once were eager participants with the leaders degenerate into spectators watching a religious show or exercise. Institutionalization of the church occurs again.

Such a repetition of occurrences indicates a distinct pattern. Whenever there is a significant emphasis on buildings, government, and programs, a decline in power occurs. However, let it be said that there is a need for structure and government in order to facilitate productive ministry. There is a need for programs and physical buildings to accommodate the congregations.

On the other hand, the manifestation of spiritual gifts without some form of scriptural direction or instruction can also be counterproductive. Consequently, as leaders, some have sought to merge sound theological concepts and practices with "principles of power." We have emphasized evangelism, discipleship, church growth, prayer, worship, unity, government, and even reconciliation of gender, race, creed, and culture. However, have these emphases become substitutes for the Spirit? Has the Holy Spirit quietly been reduced to a doctrine, a form, or simply an emotional sensation that comes in among us on Sunday morning called "The Presence?"

Contemporary Plea

In response to the aforementioned history, we will use one of Paul's

missionary journeys. Luke recorded that sometime after Pentecost, Paul met certain disciples of John the Baptist at Ephesus (Acts 19:1-7). Hearing that they knew only the baptism of John, which is a baptism of repentance, Paul presented the Gospel more accurately to them, presenting Jesus as the fulfillment of John's ministry (Matt. 3:11-12; Luke 3:15-17; 7:18-23; John 3:26-36; Acts 1:5). When Paul laid his hands on them, they received the Holy Spirit in the true Pentecostal tradition (Acts 2:4; 8:14-19; 10:44-46; 11:17; 19:4-6). Jews (Acts 4:31), Samaritans (Acts 8:14-17), Romans (Acts 10:44-46), Saul a persecuting Pharisee (Acts 9:17), an Ethiopian eunuch (Acts 8:38-39), and the 12 disciples of John the Baptist (Acts 19:1-6) all called upon the name of the Lord Jesus, and each received, as a birthright, the baptism in the Holy Spirit. Some argue that it is a reasonable conclusion from biblical evidence that tongues are the "external and indubitable proof" of their baptism in the Holy Spirit (Ervin, 1987). In fact, it appears that of all the Spirit's supernatural gifts, tongues appear first at Pentecost. The other gifts follow subsequently (Acts 2:4; 8:14-19; 10:44-46; 1 Cor. 12-14; Gal. 5).

Pentecostals believe the Spirit *dwells* in every Christian but not all Christians are filled with, or baptized in, the Holy Spirit. Being baptized in the Spirit empowers Christians with spiritual gifts, such as healing and speaking in tongues. The "baptism in the Holy Spirit," which is distinct from having the indwelling of the Spirit, is occasionally regarded as a topic particular to Pentecostals or Charismatics. However, biblical evidence clearly presents it as the norm of the Christian experience. Perhaps it is because the Baptism in the Holy Spirit is viewed in such a restricted manner that the person of the Holy Spirit and His mission is often neglected, denied, and even supplanted.

Evangelicals and Fundamentalists believe Pentecostals speak too much about the Holy Spirit at the expense of Jesus. They use the

reference in John 16:13, "For he (Spirit) shall not speak of himself." However, when the Spirit is come, He will speak as a distinct and independent Spirit but from the common agreement of the Triune Godhead. Please note, that the Spirit is the author of Scripture. When we honor the Holy Spirit, we are honoring Jesus, since He is the Spirit of Jesus (Acts 16:1).

Throughout the centuries, the Spirit has become more refined. For example, in Catholicism, the Spirit is symbolically subordinated to the ritual of water baptism. Only the bishops have the authority to bestow the Spirit. Protestants, in their reaction to Catholicism, have shifted their interest from water baptism to preaching and personal faith, with authority being centered in the Bible rather than in the church. With the emphasis on faith as distinct and prior to water-baptism, faith and preaching is exalted, and the role of baptism is decreased. The Spirit is regarded as the originator of faith, and the reality of His work in apostolic days is acknowledged, but the gifts are declared to have ceased with the apostles. Hence, in Protestantism, the Spirit becomes subordinate to the Bible, and the Bible replaces the sacraments as the principal means of grace and inspiration.

While the Catholics focus upon the sacraments and the Protestants set forth the supremacy of the Scripture, the Pentecostals react to both extremes. They shift the emphasis from the mechanical sacramentalism of the Catholics and the dead intellectual orthodoxy of the Protestantism to the experience of the Spirit. The Pentecostals have justification for their interests (Acts 2:4; 4:31; 9:31; 10:44-46; 13:52; 19:6; Rom. 5:5; 8:1-16; 1 Cor. 12:7, 133; 2 Cor. 3:6; 5:5; Gal. 4:6; 5:16-18; 1 Thess. 1:5; Titus 3:6; John 3:8; 4:14; 7:38; 16:7).

James D. G. Dunn, author of "Baptism in the Holy Spirit: A Re-examination of the New Testament on the Gift of the Spirit," claims the

Pentecostal follows the Catholic in the notion of separation of Spirit-baptism from the event of conversion-initiation, and thus, the gift of the Spirit is an experience that occurs after conversion. According to Dunn, this seems contrary to New Testament although such a pattern is alleged in Acts 8. According to Paul and Luke, baptism in the Spirit is not something subsequent to and distinct from the salvation experience or is it something which only an apostle or bishop can bring about or is it something that happened only in apostolic days. The gift of the Holy Spirit is not separate in any way from conversion.

Regardless of the theological arguments, the Holy Spirit is indispensable for the power of Christian witness. In fact, Christianity without the Holy Spirit would simply be a powerless philosophy or a wonderful idea. The Holy Spirit is God in action through His power (Mark 16:15-18; Luke 24:49). It is His mission to bring to pass all the fruits of Christ's victory, including His lordship over all things (John 14:26; 16:7-14). All that Christ accomplishes with His life, ministry, death, resurrection, and ascension must be manifest through the Church (Eph. 1:7-10; 19-23; 2:13-22; 3:6, 10). The evidence of salvation (individual and cosmic) with its privileges and responsibilities is experienced by the Church, but there must also be the pronouncement and demonstration of God's Kingdom by the Church to the world (Matt. 24:14; 28:18-20; Mark 16:15-18; John 17:14-18; 20). The reconciliation of the world to God and the privileges of His wonderful grace and power is mediated by the Holy Spirit (2 Cor. 5:18-21). He is the executive agent of the Trinity and the Mediator of all Divine purposes, strategies, and agendas on the earth.

In the Old Testament, the Holy Spirit originates, maintains, strengthens, and guides all life (organic, intellectual, and moral) toward God's ultimate purposes (God in action on the earth). Hence, the Holy Spirit is the Dispenser of "Common Grace" (Matt. 5:45; Luke 6:35). Common Grace is that general operation of the Holy Spirit whereby He, without

renewing the heart, exercises a moral influence on man so that sin is restrained and order is maintained in social life such that God's purposes are realized.

The Holy Spirit is the first person of the Trinity that we experience when we are brought into covenant with God (John 6:44; 1 Cor. 12:3). Jesus declares the necessity of being "born of water and the Spirit" (John 3:5). Spiritual regeneration is absolutely necessary for salvation (Packer, 1988). This is mediated through the preaching of the Gospel by the power of the Holy Spirit (Rom. 1:16; 10:10-15; 1 Pet. 1:12). The preaching of the Gospel, faith, repentance, and baptism in the Holy Ghost and water are the keys that unlock the door to the ultimate destiny for the repentant sinner (Matt. 16:18; Acts 2:14-41). It is the Holy Spirit who enables the believer to relate to the Son and the Father and to enter into the Body of Christ.

The Holy Spirit is involved in discipleship (John 14:25-26; 15:26-27; 16:12-15); commission (John 20:19-23); deaconate (Acts 6:3-5); evangelism (Acts 8:15-17; 8:29-39; 9:17; 10:19; 44-47); removal of prejudice (Acts 10:1-48; 11:12-17); prophetic warnings (Acts 11:28; 20:22-24); demonic opposition (Acts 13:9); validation of ministry (Acts 4:33; 15:7-9; 2 Cor. 12:12); ministerial directions (Acts 16:6-7); and validation of callings (Acts 20:28; 2 Cor. 13:3). At the meeting of the Sanhedrin, when the missionary endeavors of Peter and Paul comes under the scrutiny of the other apostles and elders, James demonstrates the significance of the Holy Spirit in counsel with the words, "It seemed good to the Holy Ghost and to us" (Acts 15:28).

The Spirit validates callings and confirms the Gospel message. This is a critical factor in understanding true apostolic authority. Contrary to ancient Roman Catholicism, Protestant reformers saw the apostolic foundation as the Gospel of Jesus Christ; and his death and resurrection are the fulfillment of the law and the only basis for salvation from sin and the granting of eternal life (Anderson, 1993). The mechanical

succession of apostolic authority that is based in direct succession back to Peter without an understanding of the witness and teaching of the first apostles is highly suspect. In fact, such a theology of the church, which is based on some kind of historical continuity with the incarnation through the first century apostles, tends to marginalize the Pentecost experience of the Holy Spirit. It raises suspicion concerning the role of the Holy Spirit in the interpretation of Scripture, as well as in the manifestation of the Spirit in the life and mission of the church. Some will agree with Charles Hodge, in chapter one of his *"Systematic Theology,"* that the Holy Spirit has no part in determining the rule of faith, but only in its application. Hence, Hodge claims the exegesis of the Scripture under the guidance of the Holy Spirit is too subjective and unreliable. However, Acts 4:33 declares that "with great power the apostles gave witness to the resurrection of the Lord Jesus." The connection between the Holy Spirit and the "great power" that gives witness to the Gospel is inseparable. Apostolic authority or succession is inseparable from Holy Spirit power, and the Holy Spirit validates the correctness of the Gospel.

In our efforts to be contextual and to relate to our audiences, we often specialize in aspects of the redemptive message and neglect to preach the full counsel of God. Each revival emphasis during the last century has exerted a significant influence upon the messages preached in the churches. The revival of principles and practices of faith, healing, deliverance, evangelism, worship, unity, and others, in fact, have influenced the preaching itinerary. This problem has been compounded during times of building projects in which concepts of covenant and personal commitments are stressed. Although the Gospel lends itself to unlimited variations, there are basic contents (Green, 1970).

Of particular interest is when Bishop Earl Paulk began preaching and teaching things concerning the Kingdom of God that the ministry

began to experience tremendous consequences (Paulk, 1984). There were significant manifestations of the Holy Spirit and unprecedented growth and expansion of the ministry. This should not be surprising since the preaching of Jesus Christ and the apostles centered on the Kingdom of God. In the preaching of the Kingdom of God, we are brought face to face with the whole revelation of God. Furthermore, the Kingdom of God is inseparable from the ministry of the Holy Ghost (Rom. 14:17).

Paul declares that God has not chosen many "wise according to the flesh," and "not many mighty, not many noble;" but He has chosen the "foolish things of the world to put to shame the wise, and God has chosen the weak things of the world to put to shame the things which are mighty…that no flesh should glory (boast) in His presence" (1 Cor. 1:26-29). These statements should not be used to dismiss the need for education and training among the saints. The Holy Spirit works with those who discipline themselves and their minds. However, the Spirit is not limited to the exploits of educational endeavors or is the validation of a minister dependent upon a doctoral degree.

Paul also writes that the "Spirit also helps in our weaknesses (infirmities)" (Rom. 8:26). This reference to "weakness" or "infirmities" is often restricted to the inability to pray effectively or to know what to pray for. There is a broader meaning here that relates to human talents, skills, and abilities. Paul declares that he came to the Corinthians in weakness, in fear, and in much trembling; and his speech and his preaching was not with persuasive words of human wisdom, but in demonstration of the Spirit and in power (1 Cor. 2:3-4). Having learned from Gamaliel, a leading authority in the Sanhedrin and a Jewish law teacher, Paul was a skilled craftsman with words and extremely knowledgeable (Acts 22:3). Yet, he did not rely upon his natural abilities to reason or to speak (1 Cor. 2:13). He prayed for the right words to use in order to make known the mystery of the

Gospel (Eph. 6:19). Paul knew that human abilities or strengths are at best weaknesses and infirmities (Phil. 3:3-7) in relation to the needs of the Kingdom. He knew that human inabilities, whether they are experiential, verbal, intellectual, or physical, are compensated by the Spirit. It is the Holy Spirit that enables the minister to preach, teach, plan, set goals, and accomplish them. Indeed, we do not know what to pray for as we ought, and we do not know how to accomplish spiritual ministry either (Rom. 8:26). Regardless of human ability, without the Holy Spirit, the ministry of the preacher is simply "persuasive speech of human wisdom." The Holy Spirit is the "compensator" for all our natural and even spiritual shortcomings.

Even though the reception of the Holy Spirit affects the believer's intelligence, it does not do so intellectually. With the help of the Spirit, we can understand the Scripture and spiritual matters, but the Spirit does not alone, independent of the Word, provide that understanding. Dr. Ern Baxter, an outstanding teacher and theologian who understood the Pentecostal and the historic Church traditions, would often state in his lectures that believers need their spirits and their minds baptized in the Holy Spirit. Such a statement gives clear support to the fact that the presence of the Holy Spirit in the lives of the believers is no substitute for sound doctrine. The intelligence of the Spirit is to be found in the Word. Hence, there must exist a proper relationship between the Word and the Spirit (Matt. 22:29).

Is the Holy Spirit being nudged out the work of the Church today? Does it still "seem good to the Holy Spirit and us" in our decisions and choices? Is baptism in the Holy Spirit considered the norm or the exception of the salvation experience? Is the Holy Spirit the validation of ministry or is it public consensus? How much priority is given to His presence in the corporate meetings of the church? Has the need for church structure, ministry productivity, and congregational growth compromised our sensitivity to the Spirit?

While these questions are important considerations, our rightful focus should be in getting wrapped up with the Spirit personally. In seeking to understand His authority, function and expression, remember that the Holy Spirit is not a doctrine, a feeling, or simply a presence. The Holy Spirit regenerates us and generates faith in the Word of God. He illuminates the believer with the knowledge of God (Rom. 1:21; 1 Cor. 2:14; 2 Cor. 4:4; Eph. 5:8). The Holy Spirit renews the mind making it capable of receiving insight unavailable to the unregenerated mind (1 Cor. 2:14-16). Ultimately, He will enable us to accomplish what Christ Jesus has already finished, and that's enough!

CRISIS 2

Absence of a Philosophy of Ministry

An integral relationship exists between the Word and the Spirit. The Spirit is the power of God, and the Word represents the intelligence. The Word (intelligence) without power (the Spirit) is dead intellectuality, and the power without the Word is fanaticism. The Word contains the restraints, instructions, and counsels of the Lord while the Spirit provides the dynamic necessary to accomplish the details. Such a spiritual integration is indispensable for the productivity of every church. The separation of power from instruction is detrimental to growth and productivity.

This idea of an integrated approach to ministry reveals the need for both instruction and power. Notwithstanding the outpouring and demonstration of the Spirit within a congregation, the absence of operational details is the breeding ground for conflict, competition, and crisis. Considering all the differences in personalities, objectives, values, and experiences among people, there must be some resident norm that connects all of the parts together. Such a norm should be outlined in a document referred to as a "philosophy of ministry," or ministry philosophy, which provides the boundaries, interests, expectations, values, and operational criteria for the entire faith team. A ministry philosophy refers to principles, concepts, and values used to make decisions, establish priorities, exercise influence, and measure effectiveness that guide and motivate the entire faith family.

When such principles and concepts are internalized, they become the basis for assumptions, decisions, conduct, and attitude. People must be given the opportunity to cooperate and participate in a mutually productive manner, and this is possible when they know what is expected of them.

It must be understood that methods change while principles are con-

stant. In other words, while the strategies for ministry accomplishments may vary, there must remain irrevocable principles that must be biblically based. While there may be some similarity between a secular corporation and a church, the latter must be established upon principles such as integrity, honesty, fairness, loyalty, faithfulness, excellence, patience, love, and other foundational truths that are revealed in Scripture.

Ministry philosophies may be simplistic or complex, complete, or in development. However, if the purpose of the ministry philosophy is to be realized, all levels of the faith community under its influence must comprehend it. Once again, people are more effective when they know the parameters, values, goals, and requirements of a ministry.

A basic ministry philosophy should at least include principles and details that relate to the following:

- job descriptions
- ministry values
- evaluation of effectiveness
- decision making
- conflict resolution
- income resources and expenditures

Structure is the process of accomplishing the aforementioned objectives. There must be a system of allocating rights and duties while creating channels of cooperation. Structure is shared commitment and is not simply the concern of a limited minority called "leaders." It is a majority function that should provide for the involvement of people. Structure should be adaptive and capable of responding to an ever-evolving ministry. After all, structure is to facilitate function. Structure must also embody character. Integrity, fairness, equity, humility, courtesy, love, nurturance, and patience are indispensable for the effectiveness of any governmental process.

Even though there are various governmental forms, it is advisable to consider a structure that advocates a plural form of leadership rather than a hierarchical form. The mutual recognition of gifts and callings can provide a healthy atmosphere for ministry. Such an idea does not dispense with the necessity of "a leader," but it can create an atmosphere of trust and cooperation when there exists multiple leaders with a mutual respect and recognition of a variety of gifts and callings.

Finally, structure should facilitate the involvement of people regardless of such distinctions as race, socioeconomic status, age, and gender. This is especially true regarding gender where women are often excluded from leadership. Creation order and redemptive history reveal men and women functioning equally in the Kingdom of God and the Church. When women are excluded from their biblically-affirmed positions as leaders, the consequences are generally expressed in deficiencies in decision-making, discernment, counsel, insight, and in the overall character of the ministry function.

When these and other areas of concern are understood and internalized, then crisis resolution can become a possibility.

CRISIS 3

Compromised Preaching Agendas

P reaching is indispensable for salvation, for they cannot hear without a preacher. Whenever the word "preach" is used in Scripture, it is in association with Christ, Word, Gospel, or Kingdom. Preaching is intended to inform the mind, stir the emotions, reinforce the faith, and command the will. Hence, the content of preaching ultimately becomes a visible reality among the congregation. That is, the word becomes flesh, or alive, and dwells among the people.

Many churches, in an effort to be relevant and contextual, suffer from the subtle dangers of a legalistic mixture and compromise of the Gospel. The Galatian and Colossian epistles reveal such possibilities. Efforts to revive the demands of the law and the additions of other tenets, or requirements, create a syncretism, or a cocktail gospel. However, only the Gospel is "the power of God unto salvation" (Rom. 1:16).

In addition, an obvious danger of overspecialization or marginalization of the Gospel message can be equally problematic; for example, whenever the principles of faith are emphasized at the expense of the full counsel of God. We know that it is possible to promote faith, healing, deliverance, and any other singular aspect of gospel provisions and omit reference to the comprehensive message. In fact, it is possible to emphasize the Second Coming at the expense of the accomplishments of the First Coming. It is perhaps preferable to preach the First Coming and make reference to the Second, for it is in the First that we obtain salvation and the full counsel of God through the sacrifice of Jesus Christ and the subsequent omnipresence of the Holy Spirit.

So, if we consider preaching as the initiator to the salvific whole, then

we must look to scripture for a guide. Paul reveals the strategy of his preaching. He always included knowledge, revelation, doctrine, and prophecy in his messages (1 Cor. 14:6). Such a strategy provides for the expression of both Word and Spirit. Knowledge is a product of experiences both in the natural and spiritual realm. Revelation is Divine disclosure and provides insight into the person, nature, character, and purposes of God. Doctrine represents human effort, hopefully inspired, to encapsulate truth into a manageable and applicable form. Prophecy is inspired speech that should reveal Divine purposes and intentions. While these definitions are not exhaustive, they reveal a need to constantly evaluate the content and intent of preaching.

Essentially, whenever there is a compromise of the biblical pattern of preaching, there are consequences in the attitude and operational behavior of the congregation.

CRISIS 4

Advertisement of Ministry

piritual marketing centers on the concept that ideas, beliefs, and practices must be promoted or advertised for effectiveness. Public billboards, magazines, and other commercial and networking outlets serve as tools of public exposure. However, in our contemporary faith culture, public relations, as opposed to simple promotion, has become a vital aspect of ministries and churches. The difference lies in the attempt to create sincere connectedness between people, and it requires both practical and spiritual sensitivity. In addition, congregations must demonstrate a balance between having a positive public image and exemplifying lives of Kingdom effectiveness. In the past, many churches sought growth, size, even glamour as the measure of success, yet authentic ministerial greatness is distinct from that.

Christians must never forget that "if two of you shall agree on earth as touching on anything," and "whenever two or more are gathered" in His name (Matt. 18:19-20), the ultimate result is the response of the Almighty. Thus, in the process of promoting a ministry and becoming visible, the original purposes and priorities must be maintained.

Let us examine the temptation of the Lord Jesus (Matt. 4:1-11; Luke 4:1-13) for some very interesting observations in reference to spiritual marketing. Satan offered things to the Lord that were intended to connect to some deficiency or weakness, such as pride, ignorance, greed, or arrogance. However, the temptations found nothing in the Lord upon which to attach themselves. In a sense, the temptations were intended to prepare and design ministries against similar attacks. The propositions were intended to direct the life and ministry of the Lord after His ascension.

In the life cycle of every ministry, there will be moments of decisions.

There will be times of extreme vulnerability to suggestions and alternatives. This is especially true when deficits are evident. Leaders seek to compensate and take advantage of opportunities to redesign a ministry for the sake of visibility, accessibility, productivity, and popularity. As noble as these efforts may appear, it is important to remember the Biblical essence of the work. Indeed, progression demands change and restructuring of ministry outlets and functions. Meanwhile, beware of spiritual marketing that simply seeks to promote visibility, popularity, and even success while sacrificing the original vision, which will lead to authentic, ministerial greatness: the glorification of the Lord Jesus Christ and the promotion of His Kingdom.

CRISIS 5

Emulation Without Revelation

ince we seek to duplicate that which we admire, emulation is a high form of respect. To strive to achieve levels of excellence in life by shadowing the noble character and performance that is seen in others is an especially noble aspiration. However, a subtle temptation exists for ministers and every individual who emulate others without revelation or calling.

The prologues to two verses of Scripture have always demanded my attention in this regard. From Jude 1:6, it reads, "And the angels who left their habitation..." Paul in Philippians 3:13, stated, "...this one thing I do..." These verses are striking because they represent an exhortation to faithfulness to my own gift and calling. First, Angelic beings abandoned their assignment; the result is that they remain in darkness until judgment. Second, Paul declares faithfulness to his calling, and in this, we all should desire to be consistent.

Paul exhorts Timothy to "follow me as I follow Christ" (1 Cor. 11:1). However, there are boundaries to emulation. For example, the seven sons of Sceva sought to emulate the ministry of Paul, but they had disappointing results (Acts 19:14-15). Paul makes reference to some who seek to teach the law without understanding and abilities. So, we can see that emulation without revelation is rarely profitable. Revelation speaks of Divine enablement, such as gifting, wisdom, knowledge, and understanding. It establishes the distinctions in life and ministry. In fact, Paul speaks of understanding given specifically to him and other apostles that was denied others (Rom. 16:25-27; Eph. 3:1-7; Col 1:26-29).

Gifts and callings express of the sovereignty of God to delegated responsibilities. They express Divine grace as demonstrated through human vessels. Each one possesses its own job description. Whether

it is the five-fold ministry, which includes apostle, prophet, evangelist, pastor, teacher (Eph. 4:11), or any area of responsibility, there are guidelines and boundaries of operation. According to the grace and measure of faith, every member of the body of Christ has an assignment, and all of these functions contribute to productivity of the whole group.

Paul speaks of the Church as a body with many members that fit together perfectly (I Cor. 12:12-14). Each body part or member contributes to the entire body. I like to see this as the principle of cooperation and not competition. Church members should not strive between themselves. To use a symbolic example: If the feet are competing with the hands and the eyes are demanding superiority over the ears, then confusion results because each is interdependent and essential to optimal functioning. Let's look at a practical example: If we enter a restaurant, and the host, waiter, cook, and cashier are all striving to serve at the table, then there is confusion resulting from the departure of the job description of each worker. It is also an indication that the host, cook, and cashier think that the waiter's job is more important than theirs, yet each one is needed for the restaurant to function well.

Similarly, competition in spiritual matters brings confusion. In a church body, if the musicians are competing with the youth pastors and the ushers are competing with the childcare workers, then people will become confused. Hurt and emotional injury will also come in some manner as well. Ultimately, needs won't be met and ministry will not truly occur either. So, before you know it, the church that began with the most wonderful of visions and missions is off course, caught in self-maintenance as opposed to the ministry of the Gospel of Jesus and his Kingdom.

In addition to body confusion, sometimes an identity crisis will arise

in the life of an individual, leader, or ministry. This is especially true in leadership of churches when efforts are made to duplicate the success of others. To emulate the noble characteristics in other people and ministries can denote a tool of learning and growth. However, a subtle crisis arises when boundaries are crossed and leaders and even ministers abandon their own gifts, calling, and mission or vision. That is, when they seek to become something or someone they are not.

Paul reminds Timothy of the ministry that he received through prophecy when the body of elders laid their hands on him (1 Tim. 4:14). Paul encourages Timothy to be true to his own gift and calling. For in that capacity, there is the enablement to perform the task.

When the pastor seeks to become a prophet or a teacher aspires to become an evangelist, or the deacon attempts to be an apostle, then confusion will emerge, and the vision will be left behind. While the motive of such confusion may be ignorance or even a noble desire to emulate someone, the consequences are the same. We need to stay true to our own gift and calling. We should not be as the angels who left their assignments, but rather emulate Paul with these words: "This one thing I do."

CRISIS 6

Raising Money

inistry programs and projects require money to function, and tithes and offerings are common avenues for such support (Matt. 23:23; Luke 11:42; 18:12). Occasionally, a church may solicit funds for specific projects, which often demand creative fundraising programs. As such, the demand for finances beyond the usual operational expenses can cause leaders to mention money more often in their messages. A crisis occurs when these special project needs create a vulnerability to a variety of suggested finance schemes and devices.

Legitimate and illegitimate business schemes occur in the economic mainstream. They have included multilevel marketing programs, pyramid schemes, investment clubs, and interest free loans. In many instances, these same business endeavors have invaded churches. Oftentimes, members eager to yield a return on large sums of money have envisioned these plans as God-given ideas. Even leaders have embraced these plans in hopes of generating income. The crisis arises when the church endorses or aligns itself with these business ideas and schemes. While such public endorsement grants instant credibility to the plan, the integrity of the church becomes dependent upon the success of the business endeavor.

The church is distinct from any other community by reason of its origin and function. Only the church can proclaim and demonstrate salvation through its message and ministry. While the work, mission, and financial support of the church are inseparable entities, it is imperative that leaders establish guidelines for each of these functions. A lack of clarity in these areas becomes the catalyst for lawlessness and confusion among the congregation. It opens the door for all kinds of creative and innovative ideas and schemes to enter the mainstream of the church. While many of those ideas may

be fine in the marketplace, they are inappropriate within the church as a means of ministerial growth.

If a church delegates its financial integrity to external leadership, even for the purposes of raising monies for ministerial needs, a subtle danger will arise. The appeal of great provision will cause many in the congregation to look to the external group with a greater level of trust, confidence, and response than they have for the church's internal leadership and ultimately toward Christ, the provider. Eventually, the congregation will evolve into a mode of allowing that external group to be wholly responsible for monies generated into the ministry. To put it clearly, the church will become lazy in its own generation and management of monetary resources. The leadership will become a people who spend time generating persuasive appeal in order to get more money from the members; some will resort to a subtle manipulation of scriptures that will instill fear-motivated giving. Congregants may indeed give, but they will eventually do so because they are afraid not to. Scripture indicates, however, that we should give cheerfully and willingly (2 Cor. 9:7).

Raising money within the church is a matter of trust. Thus, church leadership should respond with clarity, transparency, integrity, honesty, humility, and responsibility. When a congregation and its leaders put more confidence in business schemes rather than in Jesus Christ as provider, then a crisis is very present.

CRISIS 7

Expansion of Ministry

Building programs represent challenging moments in the lifecycle of any ministry. New construction, expansions, additions, and even relocation to an existing site can present opportunities for growth and challenge. Even the best of plans can be populated with the unexpected and the unwanted. When a church decides to enter this process, careful consideration needs to be given to the motivation for a building program. Is it a Divine directive or simply a solution to meet the needs of a growing ministry? Is it a desire to escape a community that is declining economically or changing racially and ethnically? Is it a strategy to simply improve the popularity and visibility of the ministry?

Regardless of the underlying reasons, a congregation should not rush into a building program, for it increases the overhead costs – sometimes in unpredictable ways. Therefore, careful consideration should be given to possible alternative solutions to new construction/ relocation, such as multiple services, home meetings, and/or a reorganization of the ministry functions.

Pastor Dan Rhodes, an elder and engineer, has over 30 years of experience in all of the dynamics involved in construction/expansion of facilities. As a pastor, he understands the delicate relationship that exists between Divine directives, building programs, and the needs and demands of a congregation. On his website _www. DestinyNavigators.org_, he has written a very comprehensive article titled "Church Building Program: Asking the Right Questions." He poses some very fundamental questions concerning motivation, design, financing, and final outcome. Every church leadership should answer these and present the information to the congregation for discussion.

- *What is our mission?*
- *Why do you want to build or expand your present facility?*
- *Is the congregation on board with you on this project?*
- *Is the church able to pay for the construction and ongoing expenses?*
- *What congregation size do you desire?*
- *Are you thinking practically about funding, accommodations and so forth?*
- *What do you want the building to look like inside and outside?*
- *Are you pleased with the architectural design?*
- *Have you planned a grand opening and celebration with the people in mind?*

These and many other questions help to focus attention upon details and considerations that are often overlooked. They also help to anticipate challenging moments and perhaps avoid unnecessary difficulties.

In addition to these questions, two major considerations involve motive and alternative. Motive speaks of the fundamental basis for the activity. It embraces the spiritual and the natural. The natural factors include the desire for more visibility and accessibility to the public, space sufficiency, external structural appearances, and the status of the surrounding community. Similarly, sometimes community indicators, such as the race, economics, crime, and a declining congregation base, play a pivotal role in the decision to relocate a ministry.

The spiritual considerations represent the overall concept of the work and mission of the church as a representative of the consciousness of God in a community. It also includes original vision statements, objectives, and prophetic directives given during the earlier phases of

the ministry. While necessity and the desire for accessibility, visibility, and even popularity may be compelling factors, the decisions to build/expand/relocate should also embrace vision and fundamental objectives of the ministry. Although the times have changed, we must remember that the early church was hidden in catacombs and homes, and its strength resided in its message and spiritual power, not in its building or location.

Finally, alternatives should be considered such as multiple services, house meetings, and the diversification of ministry functions into different time slots. Sunday is not the only day one can worship, for we should seek and serve the Lord every day. For that reason, when a facility is maximized on one specific day, then alternative times may prove to be viable. When the motive and alternatives are considered, then the compelling concern is the God factor. In other words, what has God revealed or shown you regarding construction or expansion plans? The Divine command to "arise and build" (Nehemiah 2:20) is a greater motive than the demands for visibility, accessibility, popularity, and more space. It is wonderful, although challenging, when revelation and construction/expansion are partners.

CRISIS 8

Restoring the Fallen

roverb 14:4 declares that where there are no oxen, the crib is clean; but much increase is by the strength of the ox. That is, if the animal is departed, its dwelling place is clean, but the animal is such an asset that it may be worth the mess. Thus, if you want growth and expansion, then you have to be willing to deal with the issues that come along with it.

Because literature of a proverbial nature is metaphorical, this verse can also relate to the association that exists between people and problems. Where there are no people, there are no problems. If the Church had no people, there would be no problems. However, the Church is comprised of people (believers), and they struggle with problems and sin. The effectiveness of any ministry is measured by its willingness and ability to manage people and their mess, or sin.

A Basic Theology

At the point of creation, God did not design humanity to sin. Rather, mankind was created in the image of God and constituted to live in righteousness. Sin is actually a contradiction to true human nature and is the expression of humankind acting in a manner unbecoming to being human. Yet, sin entered the created order because of the transgression of one man, Adam. (Rom. 5:18-21). This transgression was and remains comprehensive, affecting the spirit, soul, and body. It is also progressive in its effect upon succeeding generations.

Because sin occurred, God initiated "a program" for the recovery of humankind and all creation. Salvation is the process by which humanity is taken from depravity to ultimate destiny. It is spiritual, psychological, and behavioral. The process is mediated through regeneration, restoration, and restructuring. So, by one man's disobedience (Adam),

many were made sinners, so then by one man's obedience (Jesus), many are made righteous (Romans. 5:18-21).

Jesus is the advocate for humanity, and it is he who facilitates this recovery program and process. He also inaugurates the continuation of this recovery through the Church, a therapeutic community. As the Church, in fact, we should view ourselves as the ongoing incarnation of Jesus, ordained to declare the ideal of Divine purposes and minister to those who fall short of those standards. That is, through the Church, God expresses principles, standards, and patterns of righteousness that should be emulated in patterns of thought and behavior. We, the Church, are the representatives of the consciousness of God. The business of the Church is helping humanity seek and receive redemption from sin through Christ.

- The word "sin" is typically used in a generic way as inclusive of wrongdoing and lawlessness. There are two words for "sin": First, there is "hamartia," a missing of the mark; a principle or source of action, or an inward element producing acts (Rom. 3:9, 5:12-13, 20; 6:1-2; 7:7). It is also viewed as a governing principle or power (Rom. 6:6) and an organized power, acting through the members of the body. Although the seat of sin is in the will, the body is the organizing instrument.
  The focus here is on what you failed to do what character you lack (i.e. love, patience; insight).

- Second, is "hamartema," an act of disobedience to Divine law. The focus here is on what you actually did (i.e. lie, steal).

John 1:29 says, "Behold the Lamb of God, who taketh away the sin (not sins) of the world." This singularity is significant and means a condition of sin or a course of sin. Hence, Christ's death takes away, not the tendency to miss the mark or to act unrighteous, but

the estrangement or the offense between God and humankind is removed. Thus, while humans may still miss the mark, they are no longer estranged or separated from the Creator.

Ephesians 2:12 speaks of Gentiles being "aliens," "strangers," "having no hope," "without God in the world," and "who were far off." This represents the state of humankind through Adam without Christ. Now in Ephesians 2:13-15, Paul says the Gentiles are "made near" by the blood of Christ, for He Himself is their "peace" and has abolished the "enmity." Why has the Lord done this? So that He might reconcile both (Jew and Gentile) to God and put to death the enmity, the separation, the offense. This conveys what Christ's death accomplished.

A Consistent Problem

The epistles reveal some typical examples of the human tendency to miss the mark. For example, there was Diotrpephes (3 John 9), Hymenaeus (1 Timothy 1:20; 2 Timothy 2:17), Alexander the Coppersmith (2 Timothy 4:14), Demas (2 Timothy 4:10), Euodias and Syntyche (Philippians 4:2) and a host of individuals characterized by Paul (2 Timothy 3:1-18). Each of these individuals contributed to the "daily cares of the churches" (2 Corinthians 11:28). They challenged the ministry of the apostles (2 Corinthians 11-12); contradicted sound doctrines (Galatians 1:6-9; Colossians 2:4-8); involved themselves in immorality and unethical behavior (1 Corinthians 5:1-7); and sought to disrupt productive patterns of operation in the churches (2 Timothy 4:3-4; 1 Timothy 4:1-3). Such historic problems have contemporary companions, for there remain individuals who lose track of God's direction and purpose in their lives. Part of the effectiveness of the Church hinges upon its willingness and ability to manage, help, restore, and forgive such individuals.

A Proper Diagnosis

Spiritual matters can often masquerade themselves in natural pat-

terns of behavior. For example, unbelief disguises itself as skepticism and procrastination. So, it is important to recognize not only symptoms, but also causes, because an appropriate diagnosis precedes an effective treatment. That is, there must be an appropriate determination of motive, extenuating circumstances, and influence of an occurrence. This is called "context." Is it an initial or repeated offense? Does the problem only affect the individual or does it have a corporate influence? Is it a matter of ignorance, lack of experience, or an intentional issue? Is it a character flaw, a spiritual matter, or a circumstantial occurrence?

There must be an appropriate categorizing of people according to their acts, deeds, and motivations. Some are the enemies of God who oppose Divine will and purposes (Acts 13:6-11). Some are the enemies of the Gospel who, through either ignorance or knowledge, distort the truths of Scriptures (Romans 11:28; 2 Peter 3:16). Similarly, there are those who oppose themselves and do not comprehend why they were created or the divine intentions of their bodies (2 Timothy 2:25). Therefore, irregularities in behavior may have a variety of causes.

Because sin is multidimensional and far-reaching, distinctions must be made between mistakes that affect the individual alone from those involving others (Luke 15:11-32). For example, Paul writes that the hypocrisy of the Jews provoked the Gentiles to blaspheme God (Rom. 3:17-24). Likewise, it is necessary to distinguish between things done out of ignorance form those done with knowledge (1 Tim. 1:13; Psalms 19:12-13; John 9:41; 2 Peter 3:5). Paul acknowledged that his persecution of the Church was done out of ignorance while Peter spoke of people who were willingly ignorant. This association of judgment and the character of sin is established by the Lord in dealing with the Pharisees (John 9:41). It is important that motive, influence, and consciousness be considered in an assessment of the dimension of the sin.

When administering either harsh reprisals or shallow reprimands, the person's belief system that contributed to such behavioral patterns should be examined. In fact, it would be wise to also examine an individual's doctrine and traditions for their ability to promote hypocrisy, deceit, and lawlessness. For instance, Saul's persecution of the church was based upon his convictions and doctrines.

An Appropriate Treatment

Finally, we, as the Church, need spiritual elders to help in the maturation process. The process of restoration and reconciliation should be entrusted in the hands of able and proven leadership. Compassion, integrity, experience, and revelation are indispensable, and young Christians often need the guidance that an elder can provide. In addition, the worthiness of every individual must be constantly kept in mind as he or she struggles with sin. A seasoned, loving elder can often show the proper tension between "rules and regulations" and the revelation of the Spirit. While written laws should not be entirely set aside, there must always be a place for the Spirit to reveal purposes and designs that may not always be written. Remember, while the "letter killeth," it is the Spirit that gives life (2 Cor. 3:6).

Lastly, confidentiality is mandatory in the process, particularly if a church group is involved with counseling and helping someone move beyond a habitual sin. Sometimes there is a time to "rebuke before all" (1 Timothy 4:20) and bring some kind of correction to a whole congregation or even an individual before the group. At other times, we must hold all things in confidence. Knowing when to make something public and when to conceal is a matter of discernment. Oftentimes, a process of recovery is aborted simply because of public exposure. Matthew 18:15-16 makes mention of going to someone in secret. The prophet Nathan was sent of the Lord to confront David for orchestrating the death of Uriah and later marrying his widow, Bathsheba (2 Sam. 11:1-27; 12:1-23). The prophet confronts David

privately, and David's repentance is most genuine (2 Sam. 12:13). However, the prophet Samuel publicly exposes the rebellion of Saul (1 Sam. 15:10-30). While public exposure can provoke shame, guilt, and embarrassment, the indiscriminate use of such a strategy may not always produce the desired results.

With a proper diagnosis of spiritual sickness, there can be a productive treatment. As a result, there can be life and ministry after sin.

CRISIS 9

A New Form of Idolatry

I dolatry involves the distortion of truth either ignorantly or intentionally. Idolatry has commonly been referred to as the worshiping of other gods (Exod. 20:4-5; Isa. 44:9-20; 46:6-7). However, a new form of idolatry emerges when lesser things replace greater things. When Israel, for instance, failed to retain the knowledge of God in their conscious, they began to perceive their own philosophies as the truth and so failed to glorify or even recognize God's will, ways or existence (Rom. 1:21-28). Therefore, we can say when Divine priorities and objectives are minimized in the mind, then we likewise reduce spiritual matters by making natural things seem spiritual.

Modern forms of idolatry are mostly theological in nature. They are expressed in obligations to religious traditions, practices, and concepts that are, when deconstructed, contrary to biblical truth. Often this emerges from preoccupation with "side issues" and lesser truths that become a substitute for the essentials of the Gospel. When these issues and concepts become the basis for divisions and factions, they become idolatrous.

A brief list of such concerns may be represented in the following questions:

- *Is God male or female?*
- *Is there a physical form of the Holy Spirit?*
- *Is supernatural healing for everybody?*
- *Does medicine violate faith?*
- *Do Christians need inner/emotional healing?*
- *Can a believer have a demon?*
- *Is anger a demon?*
- *Can believers direct angels?*
- *What was the skin color of Jesus?*

- *What is true spiritual warfare?*
- *Are women in subjection to men?*
- *Can women have charge or authority over men?*
- *Is the rapture real?*
- *When is the tribulation?*
- *Who is the antichrist?*
- *Is personal prophecy legitimate?*
- *Is speaking in other tongues the sign of the baptism of the Holy Ghost?*
- *Can a believer be under a generational curse?*
- *Is chemical addiction a spiritual problem?*
- *Is pre-marital sex a sin?*
- *Is Jesus coming any day?*
- *Will the temple be rebuilt in Jerusalem?*
- *Are the Jews more important than the Gentiles?*
- *Is tithing an Old Testament law?*
- *Can a believer listen to any form of music?*
- *What is a form of godliness without power?*
- *Are there mansions in heaven according to John 14:2?*
- *Can a believer marry an unbeliever?*
- *Is abortion always murder?*
- *Is prosperity for all believers?*
- *Is sickness a lack of faith?*
- *Is body piercing permissible?*
- *Is body sculpturing/alteration acceptable?*

Indeed, some of these are reasonable issues, and biblical answers should be sought as it relates to conformity to God's will. However, when these issues become the source of division and strife, the focus of Christianity shifts from making disciples of nations to debates over theological issues.

Christianity is not simply the deliverance from self-centered preoccu-

pations, fears, resentments, inner conflicts, pride, anger, guilt, emptiness, meaningless, frustrations, tensions, materialism, and greed. Christianity is also not simply escaping failure, sickness, disease, and unhappiness. All of these are byproducts of something much more significant: Jesus Christ's death for the remission of all sin so that everyone would be restored to the Father.

However, when the concern and focus of ministry and its subsequent programs are upon individual salvation and gratification without a global awareness, then the message is void of biblical wholeness. The result will eventually be a return to a Christianized self-centeredness and, therefore, a congregation with theological dysfunction. Indeed, individual salvation may be the center of God's will, but it is not the circumference. While there is a concern for individual needs and gratification, there must be the development of a belief system that focuses on the truth of God's power and love to deliver the lost. Ultimately, the focus should be on what others' need in order to be made right with God, not on what we think we need to know in order to be right in a debate or in our own minds.

CRISIS 10

Serious Negligence

F aith is not simply a religious concept, but rather it is integrated into every aspect of human existence. Our convictions, motivated by our faith, are the architects of our perspectives, values, decisions, and activities. Similarly, Christians' conviction has traditionally been the source of such belief systems within the church. However, the focus of the church has shifted, which has likewise affected its testament. This is especially true of today's much-neglected emphasis on the resurrection of Jesus Christ.

In the New Testament, the Gospel contains the entire Christ event and certainly the death and resurrection. Still, the resurrection itself, like no other Christ event, encapsulates the Gospel. In examining the early Christian message of the apostles, it is clear that the focus was on the resurrection. The first evangelists proclaimed that the resurrection of Christ secured salvation, forgiveness, and the gift of the Holy Spirit.

Today, most material written on Christology deals with the life, ministry, miracles, and death of Jesus. In fact, the two primary emphases are the birth of Jesus and the death of Jesus. However, the incarnation and the crucifixion are not the whole of the Christ event. Without the resurrection, the Gospel would not be good news. The resurrection is the event around which all other theological consideration must revolve. Let us consider this carefully.

First, the crucifixion reveals the cost of our salvation while the resurrection demonstrates its power. Without the resurrection, the crucifixion would have been an obscene tragedy. The resurrection, you see, gives meaning to the crucifixion of Jesus Christ. Otherwise, he was just a great man who died in a very unseemly execution. The crucifixion shows us the end dimension of a righteous life while the resurrection initiates a new beginning to spiritual living. Indeed,

because of the resurrection, God remains with humanity through the omnipresence of the Holy Spirit.

Let us look at the cross next. While the cross is certainly important to Christians, everything about the cross is actually deficient. The cross put an end to the fallen order of Adam (Rom. 6:6); it assures that we will crush the head of Satan (Rom. 16:20); and it crucifies the lone believer (Jesus) for the sake of the world. If our theology simply takes people to the cross and not to the resurrection, it is a deficient theological journey. Resurrection is positive since all of the results and benefits are made available to carry on life victoriously. This is by no means minimizing the cross, but we must see Jesus Christ resurrected and crowned with glory, at the right of the Father, and as the immortal King – the ultimate results of the resurrection.

When Christian theology has attempted to address the resurrection in its historical consideration, it has been through apostolic arguments as a defense of the historical accuracy of the event to prove the deity of Jesus and as a validation of the expected bodily resurrection of believers after death. The predominance of Paul's reference to the resurrection of Jesus is not to the future bodily resurrection of Christians. Instead, Paul's emphasis is that anyone who is receptive to faith in Jesus can be spiritually raised to "newness of life" (Rom. 6:4-5) by the resurrected life of Jesus. Essentially, Paul emphasized the present availability of life in Christ.

New Testament theology emphasizes that the promises of God are now realized in Jesus Christ. Christian theology looks back to the "finished work" of Jesus (John 17:4; 19:30). We should preach the first coming and make reference to the second, and not the reverse. It is not what is coming, but that it is done.

When you neglect the resurrection, you neglect the significant

moment of release of the Holy Ghost. According to the theology expressed in Acts of the Apostles, the fundamental place in salvation history is to be assigned to the resurrection of Jesus. It becomes clear that it was neither the life of Jesus nor His teachings or even His sacrificial death that formed the emphasis in the early Christian proclamation. The resurrection of Christ was the proclamation of the early Church, and therefore, it should be the same today.

REFERENCES

Anderson, R. S. (1992). *The Praxis of Pentecost: Revisioning the Church's Life and Mission*. Pasadena, California: Fuller Seminary Press.

Baxter, Ern (1995). *A Daring Biblical Approach to God's Agenda for the Church*. Shippensburg, Pennsylvania: Destiny Image Publishers.

Burgess, S. M., & MacGee, G. B. (1996). *Dictionary of Pentecostal and Charismatic Movements* (9th printing ed.). Grand Rapids, Michigan: Zondervan Publishing House.

Conn, C. W. (1977). *Like a Mighty Army: A History of the Church of God*, 1886-1976 (Rev. ed.). Cleveland, Tennessee: Pathway Press.

Dunn, J. D. (1970). *Baptism in the Holy Spirit. A re-examination of the New Testament teaching, etc.* Philadelphia, Pennsylvania: Westminster Press.

Destiny Navigators- Church Consulting & Ministry Navigation. (n.d.). *Destiny Navigators- Church Consulting & Ministry Navigation*. Retrieved August 2, 2012, from http://www.DestinyNavigators.org

Ervin, H. M. (1987). *Spirit-Baptism: A Biblical Investigation. Peabody*, Massachusetts: Hendrickson Publishers.

Green, M. (1970). *Evangelism in the Early Church*. London: Hodder & Stoughton.

Harrell, D. E. (1975). *All Things Are Possible: The Healing & Charismatic Revivals in Modern America*. Bloomington, Indiana: Indiana University Press.

Hodge, C. (1887). *Systematic Theology*. New York: C. Scribner.

Kydd, R. (1984). *Charismatic Gifts in the Early Church* (4th printing, August 1997 ed.). Peabody, Massachusetts: Hendrickson Publishers.

Packer, J. I. (1958). *Fundamentalism and the Word of God: Some Evangelical Principles*. Grand Rapids, Michigan: Eerdmans Publishing Company.

Paulk, Earl. (1984). *Ultimate Kingdom*. Atlanta, Georgia: K-Dimension Publishers.

Paulk, Earl, & Rhodes, Dam. (2000). *Theology for the New Millennium*. Atlanta, GA: Earl Paulk Ministries.

Sweet, W. W. (1944). *Revivalism in America, Its Origin, Growth and Decline*. New York: C. Scribner's Sons.